Reiki

A complete guide to Reiki healing, the human energy field, and improving your health with Reiki

Table of Contents

Introduction

Thank you for choosing this book on the topic of Reiki healing!

Throughout the following chapters, you will learn all about Reiki, how it was developed, how it works, what it can be used for, the different levels of Reiki healing, and much more!

This book includes several step-by-step instructions for different Reiki healing procedures. You will learn not only how to heal your own physical and emotional pains, but also the pains and illnesses that impact other people.

At the completion of this book you will have a good understanding of Reiki healing, and the many ways in which it can improve your life!

Once again, thanks for taking the time to read this book, I hope you find it to be helpful!

Chapter 1: Learning About Reiki and the Man Behind It

It was in the 1800s when Reiki was discovered in Japan by Dr. Mikao Usui. Usui was a Buddhist monk who came from a family of doctors. He always envisioned the development of a large community of healers, and he felt that if he could create an energy healing system, his vision would ultimately come to fruition. And so, he worked on combining religious practices, energy theories, and the study of medicine with high hopes of developing such a system.

Usui attended a spiritual experience on Mount Kurama in Kyoto, Japan, where he encountered vivid images of sacred symbols etched on rocks. He ultimately used them as his Usui Reiki symbols. Soon thereafter, after conducting thorough research, he established a healing clinic and a school for Reiki in the city.

Initially, Usui practiced Reiki on himself and then eventually practiced it on family members and close friends until he began applying it on strangers. Over the course of time, Usui's Reiki system seemed to be spreading like wildfire as people from different places – both near and far – did not mind traveling to Japan to receive the Reiki healing from him personally.

Chujiro Hayashi and Hawayo Takata should also be given credit for exerting an effort to learn and discover more about Reiki. Their interest in Usui's system led to its further popularity that reached the western world.

But what exactly is Reiki?

Reiki is a term derived from two words, namely, "rei" and "ki." Rei means Divine Wisdom or Higher Power and "ki" means the life force energy. A Reiki session consists of transmitting life force energy to a person's key energy centers in order to get rid of blockages that are said to be the major cause of all illnesses.

Reiki can be received by anyone experiencing any type of health issues – whether it is an emotional, mental, or physical issue, regardless of the severity.

Those who have received the healing power of Reiki can affirm that it can heal a person completely. It can minimize symptoms, it can shorten healing periods, and can even prevent a person from requiring major surgeries or treatment. In other words, Reiki helps a person extend their life and be free from pain and stress.

Now that you have started reading this book, I would like to believe that you are interested not only in knowing more about Reiki, but also in learning how to heal people using this system. Before you become a student of Reiki, you must remember that you have to put your one hundred per cent commitment to learning it. You have to be a patient student as you have to undergo several processes before you can become an expert in Reiki healing.

The first process is to visit spiritual, wellness, and healing centers until you find the right Reiki Master for you. Your master can actually be any Reiki Master but, it is beneficial to find someone who you are compatible with.

The second process is to attend a ceremony that lasts for a maximum of two days. The program will consist of the following activities:

1. Receiving Reiki attunements

2. Familiarizing yourself with the Reiki history

3. Understanding the Reiki principles

4. Learning how to conduct self-healing

5. Learning how to heal others

6. Applying Reiki as part of your lifestyle.

The third process involves taking a pledge to continue the Reiki practice for twenty-one days. It is during this period that you mentally, emotionally, and physiologically experience the impact of Reiki.

In the following chapters, you will be further enlightened about these three processes.

Chapter 2: The First Process: Finding a Reiki Master

In the previous chapter, it was advised that you pick a Reiki master that you feel compatible with. That way, you will have a special connection with your master and learning will be more convenient for you – in the same way that your master will find it convenient to teach you as well.

While all masters aim to reach the same goal when they teach students, they all have different teaching styles. Some masters are highly effective in teaching when they apply the traditional approach, while some are exceedingly effective using specific healing techniques.

Here are several factors that you may want to consider when choosing the ideal master for you:

1. *Check out their previous work performance and credentials*

Surf the Internet to check out the profiles of local Reiki masters – many of them will have their own websites. Check out their personal and professional information, and try to look for client feedback. Most websites mention wellness or healing centers where they have conducted sessions – consider calling those centers and dutifully conduct a background check.

2. *Find out about their beliefs and values*

It is important to find a master whose values and beliefs match yours. Observe the way they speak and act, and choose the one you are most comfortable with. Pick the master with healing approaches and a spiritual philosophy that you most agree with.

In other words, choose someone whom you think will succeed in inspiring and enlightening you. Pick someone who will wash away your doubts and hesitation. Most importantly, choose someone whom you think will be able to ultimately bring out the best in you.

3. Learn about their teaching approach

All masters, of course, teach and attune their students to Reiki. However, they have different teaching and attunement strategies.

School teachers, as everyone knows, have different approaches to teaching. This is pretty much how it goes with the Reiki masters as well. However, way back when we were still in school, we did not have the power to choose our school teachers – we felt lucky to have nice teachers and not-so-lucky when we had terrible ones. But this time, you have the power to choose your master – and you have the power to choose carefully and diligently.

There are masters who prefer a group setting, while there are those who prefer a one-on-one approach. Venues vary too. Some conduct the training at a rented wellness room, at a wellness center, or at their own homes. Of course, the venue setup varies too, depending on how the master designs it.

4. Understand the difference between traditional and non-traditional teaching approaches

Aside from the traditional Usui Reiki system practiced by many masters, there are also other Reiki methods available that are also practiced by some. But since you are a beginner, you are recommended to pick a master who applies the Usui Reiki method.

5. *Let your intuition work*

It is normal to feel confused after talking to several Reiki masters and learning about their different teaching styles and venues. That's why every time you inquire, make sure that you take down notes.

Take time to analyze all the details you have gathered. Weigh all the advantages and disadvantages. The bottom line is for you to make the right decision since you will invest a lot of your money, time, and energy here.

However, do not tend to overthink. In the event that you just feel like you are in doubt of your decision-making skills, simply trust your intuition.

6. *Engage yourself in a conversation with each Reiki master you meet*

Simply talking to a master is totally different from engaging in a conversation with a master. Merely talking will give you the first impression only but you must remember that first impression is not always accurate. As the old adage goes, "Looks can be deceiving."

That is the reason why when you are face-to-face with a Reiki Master, you have to make sure that you ask as many questions as possible. Make yourself genuinely interested in everything that they say. Choosing a Reiki Master to learn from is a big step, so make sure that you really click with a person before choosing to learn from them.

Chapter 3: The Third Process: The Initiation

I have decided to discuss the third process first because all the succeeding chapters are related to the activities that form part of the second process. In this chapter, let me enlighten you about the significance of the 21-day period, which is also known as the "initiation period," to the completion of the entire Reiki Student Program.

Understanding the Third Process

This third process is recognized as the initiation period, and lasts for 21 days for a reason. This specific number of days is traditionally applied by people on spiritual undertakings regardless of their religion. It is also believed that if you can apply a process in your life for 21 consecutive days, it means that you can definitely apply it on a daily basis as part of your lifestyle.

At the start of this initiation period, it is common for students to discover that they have health issues and hidden traumas – so, expect yourself to possibly encounter the same thing. However, in spite of having been warned, you will most likely still be surprised or shocked to discover that you have emotional or physical health issues that have never been made known to you in the past. But also do keep in mind that one of the reasons why you are undergoing the third process is because you will eventually have those health issues resolved in the long run.

How Significant is the Third Process to the Reiki Student?

When you engage yourself in the act of initiation, this basically means that you, as a student, are being admitted by your mentor into a particular practice or ceremony that symbolizes the advent of your wholehearted decision to enter into a new and better way of life.

Some Reiki students wonder if this third process is significant at all or if it is only for the sake of "formality" since it has always formed part of the entire process. This is a common query from students because of the fact that the second process entails everything that a student needs to know about Reiki. This means that after completing the second process, it is already possible to tap into the universal life force energy and begin healing any time. This leaves students wondering if there still is a reason to undergo the third process.

Well, the answer is yes because, otherwise, your Reiki master would, of course, not require it. During this process, your master will significantly transmit meditative energy to you. This process is basically all about experience. The explanation is difficult to put into words. You will only understand the impact of the third process when you allow yourself to personally experience it.

It is common to want to give up during the third process, but it's important to continue for the full twenty-one days to completely understand and feel the power of Reiki.

Chapter 4: The Second Process: Receiving Reiki Attunements

The second process talks about the reijuu ceremony that every student has to participate in. Reijuu does not promote any religious tradition or element and therefore, Reiki should never be in any way considered as a spiritual practice or even a religion in itself. Instead, Reiki should be regarded simply as a healing method. Reijuu is merely the process in which the master trains you to possess the ability to access Reiki.

This reijuu ceremony consists of six activities which we will discuss throughout this book. In this chapter, we will begin by focusing on the first activity which is "Receiving Reiki Attunements."

Am I eligible to receive attunements?

Of course, you are. There are no requirements for receiving attunements. All of us are eligible to receive them. There is no age limit. There is no required mental or physical health condition. There is no need to have a lot of knowledge about Reiki. The student can be anybody. We are all eligible for it as long as we strongly believe that Reiki has the capability to improve ourselves.

How do I prepare to receive attunements?

The first three things you must strictly do to prepare to receive attunements are the following:

1. Wear clothes that are light-colored;

2. Wear clothes that you are comfortable in

3. Make sure to drink plenty of water.

Expect to apply an enormous amount of energy during the attunement process. That's why it is important that you are in your most comfortable clothes and that you are well hydrated.

Expect to feel physically, emotionally, and mentally tired after receiving attunements. That's why after you have completed the ceremony, you will be asked to rest. You will be given enough time and space to process whatever you feel until such time that you feel recovered. During this period of recovery, oblige yourself to drink water as often as possible. Remember to prevent yourself from feeling dehydrated.

What is the attunement process?

If and when you do your own research about the Reiki system, you will most likely find yourself learning a lot about Reiki masters, their teaching strategies, and the wellness or healing centers where the training takes place. But you will never find any specific information about the attunement process. This is because the process is considered sacred and cannot be disclosed. You will only know how the process truly works once you experience it yourself.

There are, however, two types of attunement processes, namely, the in-person attunement process and the remote attunement process.

1. In-Person Attunement Process

This type of attunement process does not necessarily mean that you will undergo a one-on-one training with your master, but it is one possibility – the other being a group session.

Whether it is a group session or a one-on-one session, your master will conveniently provide the ideal attunements for you, and present to you the different healing strategies in detail, including the hand positions and symbols.

This process is usually completed over a maximum of two days, though completing it within one day is more common.

2. Remote Attunement Process

The attunement process does not necessarily have to be done in person. It can take place out of the physical plane, hence, the existence of the Remote Attunement Process. Thanks to technology, this has now been made possible.

There are various online tools that can be used to make this attunement process possible such as having sessions via Facetime, Google Hangout, and Skype, just to name a few. This means that even if the master and the student are not physically together, they can still successfully complete the attunement process.

What are the different attunement and practitioner levels?

There are three attunement and practitioner levels.

Under Level 1, the attunements you will receive consist of four varied symbols that are all pertinent for you to be able to access the Reiki system.

Under Level 2, you will receive additional attunements that consist of three more symbols. You can use those additional symbols in your own Reiki practice.

Under Level 3, you will receive additional attunements that consist of two more symbols aside from the seven other symbols you have received in Level 1 and Level 2. These additional symbols will make you capable of attuning others through the Reiki system. Level 3 is also termed as the Reiki Master Level.

Once you have received the first two attunement levels, you will be capable of healing yourself, but incapable of healing others. However, once you have completed all three levels, you will have the capability to provide attunements to others as well.

What should I expect during the healing crisis?

The healing crisis is actually your road to recovery.

After your completion of the attunement process, expect yourself to be physically, emotionally, and mentally exhausted after all the energy you have used. Such exhaustion is part of the detoxing process that will last for approximately one month from the date you have completed the entire process.

During this time, you might get bothered with how bad you feel. Among the symptoms that you might encounter are the following:

- Light headedness

- Lethargy

- Lack of appetite

- Fever

- Sinus pressure

- Cold

However, you should feel relieved to find out that you are not alone during this healing crisis, because your master will simultaneously feel the same symptoms as you do. This occurrence is taken as a sign that the entire process is truly taking effect. Furthermore, after you have recovered from such a healing crisis, you are not the only one who will benefit from it. Your master will recover also and will eventually become a more skilled Reiki master. Therefore, if and when you progress as a Reiki student, they also progress as a Reiki master.

Chapter 5: The Second Process: The Different Reiki Healing Systems

The second process requires you to familiarize yourself with the history of Reiki. In Chapter 1, you were provided with a brief background of this healing system. In this chapter, we will provide more detailed information on the different Reiki healing strategies available.

There are actually ten branches of Reiki treatments that are all based on the traditional Usui Reiki methods and symbols. Under these branches are over a thousand types of healing strategies, and there is a corresponding strategy for every specific health issue whether it is physical, emotional, or mental.

Let's discuss some of these Reiki healing strategies.

The Sacred Flame

The Sacred Flame is also referred to as the Violet Flame. It has similarities with the traditional Usui Reiki healing strategy, but it requires the student to have seven more attunements. Furthermore, it allows the master to have the full authority to create their own symbols.

Raku Kei

The Raku Kei healing system consists of self-healing methods and symbols that Usui himself did not personally pass down to his successors, but instead were retrieved from his personal archives. It is believed that he opted not to include them in training his successors because of their complexity. Nonetheless, Raku Kei has now been recognized to form part of the traditional Usui Reiki healing processes.

Karmic

In the Karmic Reiki system, the Hindu principals of karma are incorporated with the elements of distance healing in Usui Reiki Level 2. The past lives as well as the current actions of an individual are healed to ensure that they will have a better future.

Celtic

In the Celtic Reiki system, the Usui Reiki styles and symbols are incorporated with the ancient Celtic healing strategies and symbols. Oftentimes, this healing system is practiced in forests or woodsy environments, giving both students and masters a different kind of soothing feeling.

Chios Energy Healing

In the Chios Energy Healing system, aura healing strategies are incorporated with the Kundalini chakra healing techniques. However, there is no need to do yoga when performing this healing system, unlike when performing the Kundalini Reiki.

Blue Star Celestial

The Blue Star Celestial healing system originated from ancient Egyptian techniques, inspired by the star constellations seen above the pyramids. A Reiki practitioner who is interested in successfully adopting this system is advised to have a keen knowledge of the cosmologically-based healing strategies introduced by the Egyptians.

Osho Neo

The Osho Neo healing system was developed by master Rajneesh. A devoted Kundalini practitioner himself, Rajneesh decided to develop a system that combined Kundali Yoga techniques, chakra healing system principals, and traditional Usui Reiki symbols.

Kundalini

The Kundalini healing method is adapted by means of Kundalini Yoga practice, because it is through Kundalini Yoga that an individual gets to successfully access their internal energy through the seven chakras.

Rainbow

The Rainbow healing system was created by Walter Lubek and derived from the teachings of Usui Reiki Master Hawayo Takata. Lubek was one of Takata's students who attuned practitioners in Hawaii.

Karuna

The Karuna healing system was developed by William Lee Rand, founder of the International Center for Reiki Training, in 1995. This system adapts the traditional Usui Reiki method with eight additional symbols that were created based on Rand's observations of his Reiki practice. In this system, both the student and the master feel increased compassion spiritually, physically, and even mentally.

Chapter 6: The Second Process: Understanding the Reiki Principles

Do you believe that healing only becomes truly effective if and when you embody purity in your conduct, actions, and words? And in order for us to practice instilling purity within us, Usui developed several principles that would allow practitioners to have an ultimate healing experience. Usui emphasized that whatever positivity – or negativity for that matter – that is shown by our outer selves is only a manifestation of our inner selves.

The concept is to consistently recall and instill in you the five Reiki principles on a daily basis, first thing in the morning. Here are the five principles:

1. *"Just for today, I will not be angry."*

When you are angry, you have this false belief that you have a great sense of power but, in reality, your body is producing a lot of toxic stress hormones. Therefore, anger will not do you any good. It ruins your day, it ruins relationships and, worst of all, it ruins your health.

Learning to let go of anger allows you to learn how to manage your emotions. Also, instead of wasting your time getting angry, use your time wisely by pondering the reasons of your anger and thinking about how you can address them.

But what should you do to get rid of your anger?

There are people who effectively clear away their anger by chanting mantras. There are those who simply think of happy thoughts. There are also those who prefer to eat sumptuous food to help them feel good. Whichever way you choose, the important thing is to make sure that you wipe away your anger effectively.

2. *"Just for today, I will not worry."*

Have you ever heard of the law of attraction? It states that you attract what you think about. Therefore, if you constantly worry that something bad is going to happen, there is a great chance that something bad will indeed happen.

Worrying is a common trait of people in general. What most of us don't realize is the fact that worrying makes us suffer and prevents us from fully living in the present. Worrying is not something that only stays in the mind, because it also attracts negativity in the physical form. This is because our thoughts are our power. We can either think of things to worry about or things that will make us happy – what would you choose?

Have you ever heard of people writing down their sorrows on a piece of paper and then eventually burning that paper or flushing it down the toilet? This allows them to let go of their worries and helps them to focus on the positive instead.

A powerful practice is to write everything down in a diary or journal on a daily basis. Then, after detailing your sorrows, end the journal entry with at least five happy things that happened to you during the day. The happy things do not necessarily have to be big things – they can be as simple as being able to wake up healthy in the morning. The idea is to realize that there are still a lot of things to be thankful for in spite of your sorrows.

3. *"Just for today, I will be grateful."*

Being grateful is indeed a powerful positive emotion. The feeling of gratitude never fails to exude positivity and happiness.

As mentioned in Principle number 2, if and when you write in your journal about your sorrows, make sure that you also write about the things you are grateful for. Also, if you find yourself spending time worrying about bad things that you are not even sure will happen to you, why don't you also spend time being grateful about the good things that could possibly happen in your life?

4. *"Just for today, I will do my work honestly."*

One way of living a positive life is to work with integrity and to generally live with honesty. Sometimes, we feel as if nothing good is happening in our lives and it's as if our efforts are not being rewarded. If and when you feel this way, always remember that the universal law is that all good things you do will ultimately be rewarded. You may not know when this will happen but, eventually, it will happen.

5. *"Just for today, I will be kind to every living thing."*

When you show kindness to other people, it does not only bring a positive feeling to the receiver, but it also brings a positive feeling to you as the giver. This highlights the fact that if you want to feel good, all you have to do is to simply express kindness to others.

This fifth principle basically emphasizes how the Golden Rule works – you have to do unto others what you want others to do unto you.

Chapter 7: The Second Process: Understanding Chakras

At this point, you are still familiarizing yourself with the history of Reiki. That's why in this chapter, we will discuss the seven chakras starting from the crown chakra down to the root chakra.

The Crown Chakra

This chakra is located just above the head and is represented by a petal-filled violet lotus. It is referred to as the position of the Higher Consciousness and is therefore linked to your association with the universe. If you have blockages in the crown chakra, there is a high likelihood that you will feel lonely, disconnected, and depressed, among other symptoms. It will seem like you totally lack direction in life. This issue, however, can definitely be addressed by Reiki.

The Third Eye Chakra

This chakra is located between your eyebrows – also known as the third eye or the sixth sense – and is represented by an indigo lotus featuring a couple of petals. If and when your third eye is awakened, you will have a vision of what is not visible to the naked eye. If you have blockages in the third eye, you will most likely have an unreasonable fear of ghosts, and you will always find yourself worrying about the future. The blockages can also affect your ability to gather information, and to determine what is the truth. However, if you regularly practice Reiki, you will most likely awaken your sixth sense and improve your intuitive faculties.

The Throat Chakra

This chakra is located at your throat's base and is represented by a bright blue-colored lotus featuring 16 petals. This chakra concentrates on your creative expression and your ability to communicate. It is associated with both your ability to speak and your ability to listen. If you have blockages in your throat chakra, you might find it difficult to express your thoughts and feelings. At the same time, you might find it difficult to listen to others. If and when you practice Reiki on a regular basis, these blockages will be removed from the throat chakra.

The Heart Chakra

This chakra is located at the area of your heart and is represented by a green lotus featuring twelve petals. It concentrates on the feeling of love and compassion and focuses on the Holy Spirit. The blockages of this chakra are most of the time caused by betrayal, relationship breakups, and traumatic experiences, among others. These occurrences unfortunately lead to a lack of compassion and insensitivity. On the other hand, a healthy heart chakra emanates unconditional love. A harmonious heart chakra will teach you to learn self-acceptance and self-love, and eventually will allow you to express unconditional love to others.

The Solar Plexus

This chakra is located just below the rib cage around the abdominal region and is represented by a yellow lotus featuring ten petals. It concentrates on the strength of your actions and your personal power, and it also focuses on your digestive system. If you have blockages in the solar plexus, you might find yourself lacking energy, and experience health issues such as diabetes, ulcers, digestive problems, and stomach aches, among others.

The Sacral Chakra

This chakra is located between the navel and the genitals, and it is represented by an orange lotus featuring six petals. It is linked to the water element and, hence, is associated with issues regarding sexuality, reproduction, urinary function, and circulation – or those bodily functions related to liquid. Blockages of this chakra may result from traumatic sexual experiences or sexual abuse, and may lead to issues related to your movement, nurturance, pleasure, creativity, emotions, and sensory experiences. If and when you practice Reiki on a regular basis, you will have a healthy sacral chakra, allowing your sensual awareness and your sense of creativity to function well.

The Root Chakra

This chakra is located just below the spine and is represented by a deep red lotus featuring four petals. The root chakra actually represents the chakra system in its entirety. It is linked to survival or life's basic necessities such as shelter, security, and food. Blockages of this chakra may result from experiences of threats related to your survival. This then may result in health issues of the spine, insecurities, and fear of loss, among others.

Chapter 8: The Second Process: How to Conduct Self-Healing

All Reiki masters and practitioners can attest to the effectiveness of self-healing. That is why masters always make sure that it forms part of the Reiki Student Program. Among the advantages of practicing self-healing techniques on a regular basis are feeling calm and balanced, being less prone to stress, having inner peace, and having a stronger immune system, among many others. Practitioners also get to conduct some experiments in terms of coming up with new methods and techniques which they can eventually teach to their students. That's why self-healing techniques are not only beneficial to students, but also to masters as they get to discover new techniques or improve upon their old ones.

How do you prepare for self-healing?

Time and concentration are two of the most important factors needed for self-healing. Concentration doesn't necessarily mean that you have to be in a private place. The environment can, in fact, be either a private or a public place. The important thing is that you can give your one hundred per cent concentration while performing self-healing techniques, regardless of the location.

How often should you practice self-healing?

Traditionally, self-healing should be regularly practiced on a daily basis for a minimum of thirty minutes. However, as you get the hang of it, you will find yourself enjoying it so much that you will regularly go for longer than thirty minutes effortlessly. There is no limit when performing self-healing techniques. The important thing is that do it on a daily basis when possible.

What is the positive impact of practicing self-healing techniques regularly?

If you go to the gym or work out on a regular basis, you know what it means if I say that exercise improves not only your physical well-being, but also your mental and emotional health. Well, same thing happens if and when you do self-healing on a daily basis.

Self-healing techniques help to repair, balance, and cleanse body cells, organs, and tissues. These techniques heal such health conditions as sprains, muscle tensions, bruises, acute pain, bloating, nervousness, depression, anxiety, and stress, among many others.

What are the different hand positions and techniques for self-healing?

1. *Palm Over Each Eye*

   This is the first hand position that you have to perform, in which each of your palms must be placed over each of your eyes. You have to remember that your hands should be positioned horizontally and not vertically, allowing the fingertips of your middle fingers to touch.

   Among the health issues that can be addressed at this point are flus, colds, allergies, fevers, stress, anxiety, migraines, headaches, eye stress, and eye strain.

2. *Palms at the Side of the Neck*

   This is the second hand position in which you place your left palm on the left side of your neck, just below your left ear, and your right palm on the right side of your neck, just below your right ear. Again, your hands should be in a horizontal position and not vertical.

Among the health issues that can be addressed at this point are fear of speaking in public, laryngitis, asthma, heart issues, artery issues, thyroid disorders, and lymphatic disorders.

3. *Palms Placed on Breastbone or Sternum*

This is the third hand position in which your palms are placed just below your collarbone. Again, do not forget that your hands should be positioned horizontally and not vertically, allowing the middle fingertips to touch.

Among the emotional, physical, and mental health issues addressed by this hand position are anxiety, chronic stress, breast cancer, heart diseases, pneumonia, asthma, and other respiratory issues. Also, this hand position helps heal issues related to love, self-love, and relationships.

4. *Palms Placed on the Chest*

This is the fourth hand position in which your palms are placed between your stomach and your collarbone. Of course, the hands should again be positioned horizontally in such a way that your middle fingertips touch each other.

This hand position further heals the health issues mentioned in item number 3.

5. *Palms Placed on the Stomach*

This is the fifth hand position in which the palms of your hands are placed over your stomach. As you've probably guessed, your hands should be positioned horizontally – this is how your hands should always be placed throughout all the hand positions.

The health issues treated by this hand position include those associated with the kidneys, liver, and digestive tract.

6. *Palms Placed Above the Groin and Under the Stomach*

This is the sixth hand position which addresses issues related to the colon, large intestines, and small intestines, among others. The hand position is the same as at number 5, just held slightly further down the torso.

7. *Palms Placed on the Groin*

This is the seventh hand position in which the palms of your hands are placed on each side of your groin. This can address issues in pregnancy, hormones, and reproductive organs, as well as issues related to finances, safety, and security.

Level 1: Self-Healing Meditation Techniques

The very first step is to find a position that you are comfortable in. Then, gently close your eyes and begin doing the breathing exercise – slowly inhale and slowly exhale. Focus on your breath, while allowing your feet, ankles, back, hands, and arms to feel relaxed. While doing this, observe how you slowly feel a sense of calmness and peace.

Now, as you deeply inhale, put your hands together – palms tightly clasped – just below your throat and above your breasts. Continue doing deep breathing exercises while asking Reiki to free your physical and spiritual bodies from any negativity blocking your life energies. Allow your body to feel the flow of Reiki. This will help prepare you to heal yourself.

The next thing you will do is scan, observe, and improve your aura. Guide your hands as you move them around your energetic field by hovering them from one body part to another, starting at the top of your head and moving down until you reach your toes. Be mindful of how each of your body parts reacts or feels as your hands hover. You will feel amazed that you can actually feel which areas have blockages and which ones feel healthy.

Deeply breathe in and breathe out as you allow your hands to draw more attention to body parts with blockages. Using the palms of your hands, smoothen your aura by moving them in such a way that you seem to be removing the wrinkles of a blanket. This way, you are washing your body with the Reiki energy.

Now, place your hands at the top of your head, continue breathing in and breathing out, being mindful of how the energy in each part of your body gets positively stronger – starting from the top of your head down to your toes. As you breathe in, strongly imagine that you are inhaling positivity and placing positive energy in each body part. As you breathe out, strongly imagine that you are exhaling negativity to remove the blockages inside your body.

Now, gently move the palms of your hands and begin to hover from the top of your head, then down over your third eye, then move on to your ears, slowly move on to your eyes, move down to your chin, and then to just below your ears. As you do this, don't forget to inhale and exhale deeply. This technique is ideal for healing emotions, energies, glands, and tissues of the body that you have hovered over.

Next, move on to your neck and make sure that you hover around your entire neck. Then, slowly move down to your shoulders and collarbone until your palms reach your chest. As previously mentioned, always remember that your hands are positioned horizontally as you hover them.

Then, guide your palms down further to your abdomen, to your navel, and just below your navel. Continue to breathe in and out deeply.

You are now ready to move on to the lower part of your body, beginning from your hips down to your thighs and knees until you reach the tip of your toes. This technique is expected to improve energy, and heal aches, stiffness, joints, blood vessel problems, and muscular issues.

Once you reach your toes, gently tug each one of them. Then, move on to your ankles and gently massage them. Do this also to your elbows and wrists. Then, gently tug on each one of your fingers.

Do the hovering exercise all over again but, this time, freely guide your palms to hover over any part of your body – anywhere you feel like it. It is best that you hover your palms over the body parts where the Reiki energy is needed most. You will sometimes feel unsure as to where you should hover your palms. If you encounter this, I suggest that you gently rest your palms on your abdomen and strongly envision Reiki flowing through you to each part of your body, starting from your head and flowing down to your toes.

Continue this technique for as long as you feel is necessary. The important thing is that you practice this technique on a daily basis, for a recommended minimum of thirty minutes. You might think that a 30-minute practice is too long but, once you start, it's quite common to feel that a 30-minute practice is too short! Give this technique a try for yourself, and you will be amazed at how quickly the time will pass.

If and when you practice these healing techniques every day for at least 30 minutes, it means that you are healing yourself consistently. That way, you should always feel good, you will always be happy, and you will be at peace before your day even starts.

Level 2: Self-Healing Meditation Techniques

The techniques in level 1 and level 2 are more or less the same. The main difference, however, is the fact that under level 2, you have the capability to apply three symbols, namely, the Distance symbol, the Sei Hei Ki symbol, and the Choku-Rei symbol. These symbols can be incorporated in the hand positions earlier discussed, or in the hand positions that you will apply in the future.

There are many practitioners who will be satisfied with level 1 techniques and will feel no need to move on to the level 2 techniques. That is perfectly fine and there is nothing wrong with that. But if and when you desire to further improve your Reiki abilities, then it is highly recommended that you apply the three symbols in your self-healing meditation techniques. We will discuss these techniques further in the following chapters.

Chapter 9: The Second Process: How to Heal Others

Advanced Reiki practitioners have the ability to heal not only themselves, but also others. This means that once you master healing yourself, the next step is to master healing others as well.

The hand positions and healing techniques discussed in this book focus on techniques that are patterned after the traditional Usui Reiki methods. However, once you become a full-fledged Reiki practitioner, you will find yourself adjusting those hand positions and techniques based on what is convenient and effective for you and for your clients – or what is convenient and effective for you as a master and for your students.

How do you prepare your client for Reiki?

When you become a Reiki practitioner yourself, the first thing you do is to always remind your clients to come in their most comfortable clothes and make sure that they hydrate themselves.

Once you are face to face with your client and you are about to start the healing session, ask them to find a position that they are most comfortable in – it doesn't matter if they are lying down, standing up, or sitting down. Then, ask them if they have any health issues. Most of the time, when you ask about health issues, clients only state their physical illnesses, so you have to be specific in asking if they also have any mental and emotional issues. Explain to them why you are asking these questions – tell them that you want to pay extra attention to body parts that need healing the most.

How long does a healing session last?

In general, a Reiki healing session takes a minimum of thirty minutes. This, however, also depends on the needs of your clients. If ever your client has several health issues, their healing session might last longer.

Level 1: The Different Healing Hand Positions and Methods

The hand positions are basically the same as those used for self-healing. The difference lies on three additional positions that will highly focus on the feet and legs of your clients.

You have the option to either gently touch the body parts of your client, or to simply hover over each body part.

1. *Palm Over Each Eye*

    Ask your client to gently close their eyes. Place your palms over their closed eyes to heal such health issues as flu, cold, allergy, fever, stress, anxiety, migraine, headache, eye stress, and eye strain, among others.

    If you are allowed to touch the client, make sure that you do not put pressure on their face. If the client doesn't want to be touched, simply hover over their eyes.

2. *Palms Over the Temples*

    From the top of the eyes, move on to the sides of the client's face, above the temples. Hover your left palm over the left temple and hover your right palm over the right temple. This is easily done if the client is lying down and you are standing by the head of the bed, or if the client is sitting down and you are behind them. If you are permitted to touch the client, place the palms of your hands on the temples.

If you are in front of the client, then your left palm must be on the right temple, and your right palm must be on the left temple.

This hand position can heal such health issues as flu, cold, allergy, fever, hearing impairment, ear infection, stress, anxiety, migraine, headache, eye stress, and eye strain, among others. It can heal problems related to the pineal gland, pituitary gland, brain, sinuses, ears, and eyes.

3. *Palms Under the Head*

When you do this hand position, you can't simply hover over the body part. You have to cradle the head of your client, with your palms on the back of their head and your fingertips touching the back of the neck. In other words, it is best that your client chooses the lying position, in which case you are supposed to be standing by the edge of the bed where their head is positioned in order to perform this healing technique.

4. *Palms on the Neck*

To perform this hand position, you must be in front of your client. Your client may sit down, lie down, or stand up – again, it all depends on where they are most comfortable.

Position one palm on one side of the neck, just below the ear, and do the same thing on the other side. Among the issues that can be addressed by this technique are fear of speaking in public, laryngitis, asthma, heart issues, artery issues, thyroid disorders, and lymphatic disorders. In other words, it helps heal issues of the throat chakra, thyroid, vocal chords, lymph nodes, pulmonary arteries, esophagus, and lungs.

5. *Palms Placed on Breastbone or Sternum*

Place your palms below the collarbone. This technique helps heal issues of the heart chakra, breasts, thymus gland, heart, and upper lungs. Among the health conditions it can heal are anxiety, chronic stress, breast cancer, heart issues, pneumonia, breathing problems, and asthma. Since this is associated with the heart chakra, this technique can also heal issues related to passion, love, self-love, and relationships.

6. *Palms Placed on the Chest*

Place your palms on the chest, below the collarbone, but above the stomach. This is linked to the fifth hand position and therefore heals the same issues or those related to the heart chakra.

7. *Palms Over the Stomach*

Place the palms of your hands directly on the stomach. This technique heals issues associated with the solar plexus chakra or those issues related to the liver, gallbladder, kidneys, pancreas, and of course stomach. The solar plexus chakra is linked to creativity and therefore you as a practitioner should work on this if your client encounters blockages or if they lack inspiration to work on a creative project.

8. *Palms Placed Under the Stomach and Above the Groin*

This hand technique helps heal issues related to the colon, large intestines, and small intestines. One of the illnesses that it can heal is the irritable bowel syndrome.

9. *Palms Placed on the Groin*

In this hand position, the palms of your hands are side by side and are placed on top of the groin. This is linked to the root chakra and therefore can address issues with pregnancy, hormones, and reproductive organs, as well as issues related to finances, safety, and security. This can also be an additional healing technique for clients with problems related to their urinary or digestive systems.

10. *Palms Placed Over the Legs*

Place your palms over the legs and hover down to the soles of your client's feet. Some practitioners choose to give a gentle tug on their clients' heels as it helps increase their energy.

Providing the Maximum Reiki Experience

Traditionally, Reiki hand positions and healing methods are done on one side of the body only – which is the front body. However, many practitioners now believe that Reiki healing should take place on both sides – front and back – to allow clients to have the maximum experience. This is also highly recommended if your client needs intensive healing from intense physical and emotional issues.

As mentioned previously, it's okay for your client to choose the position they are most comfortable in. However, if you are conducting healing to both sides of the body, then the laying down position is the most convenient.

Level 2: The Different Healing Hand Positions and Methods

Compared to the Level 1 healing session, this second level requires you to pay more attention and exert more effort in healing your clients, most particularly in terms of providing intensive healing using the Choku Rei symbol, emotional healing, and offering remote healing if it is impossible for the client to physically visit your place.

If and when you facilitate the Level 2 healing session, you are allowed to use different symbols, but you are also given the freedom to use the Level 1 healing positions and methods. Using Level 2 symbols simply augments your capabilities to heal spiritual and emotional issues and, most importantly, they enable you to conduct distant healing sessions.

Understanding the Sei Hei Ki Symbol

Sei Hei Ki is the symbol for emotional healing. Sometimes, you will notice clients responding positively to the Reiki healing process and that they have been healed physically, but this does not automatically mean that they are healed emotionally as well. In this case, you have to make sure that you also address their emotional issues. This is because there are findings, in both fields of medicine and alternative medicine, showing that negative emotions have a strong impact on our physical health. And in order to succeed in working on this particular area, you have to apply the Sei Hei Ki symbol when you heal clients.

If you hear clients say that their physical health issues keep recurring, apply the Sei Hei Ki symbol on them right away. You can also combine this with the Chokru Rei symbol which you can apply before and after the application of the Sei Hei Ki symbol. This strategy will further strengthen the power of the entire healing process.

Understanding the Choku Rei Symbol

In order to further strengthen your ability to conduct Reiki healing, you have the freedom to apply the Choku Rei – which signifies power. This symbol is particularly applied by practitioners to help in addressing physical health issues such as terminal illnesses, injuries, surgeries, and chronic health problems.

Understanding Distance or Remote Healing Techniques

In the previous chapters, we mentioned the possibility of healing clients remotely. Now, let me explain to you two traditional methods for distance healing.

1. *The Surrogate*

    Distance healing can be done by assigning a surrogate for your client. The surrogate can be any other person – in fact, it can even be you. But the surrogate does not necessarily have to be a human being. Believe it or not, it can also be a doll, a crystal, a pen, a teddy bear, a cushion, a photograph, or any other object. In fact, it can even be a mere piece of paper on which important details about the person are all written. It doesn't matter what or who will replace the person who would like to receive healing. The important thing is that you can successfully channel Reiki to that surrogate.

    Before you begin the healing process, make sure that you have successfully communicated with Reiki your intention to use a surrogate for a particular client. To do remote healing, all you have to do is to do the exact healing techniques and hand positions mentioned in this book – but this time, perform the healing techniques on the surrogate. You have to strongly use your imagination to be able to successfully conduct the entire healing process, imagining that the surrogate you are using is actually your client.

2. *The Knee and Thigh Method*

To conduct this type of distance healing method, you are required to sit down. Your knees and your thighs will both represent the front and back of your client.

Your right knee and thigh shall represent your client's front body. Touch your right knee and imagine it to be your client's head. Slide your hand up to your right thigh and imagine half of it to be your client's upper body and the other half to be their lower body.

Now, your left knee and thigh shall represent your client's back. Touch your left knee and imagine it to be the back of your client's head. Slide your hand up to your left thigh and imagine half of it to be the back of your client's upper body while the other half represents the back of their lower body.

This method allows you to easily navigate your hands to the right positions. You might also need a strong imagination to do this successfully but, it can be a very powerful method for remote healing.

Chapter 10: The Second Process: Applying Reiki as Part of Your Lifestyle

Here are some tips on how you can incorporate Reiki into your lifestyle:

1. If problems come your way, it is normal to initially feel deeply sad and worried. If you experience this, do not get discouraged. Instead, take some time to practice Reiki healing, and focus on bringing yourself back to positivity.

2. Keep a journal to monitor your progress as a Reiki practitioner. Make sure that you update it on a daily basis. Jot down the activities you did, describe how you felt, write down the things you need to improve on, and so on and so forth.

3. Create a meditation corner in which you can display objects that are sacred to you. You may also create a meditation altar where you can display symbolic sacred objects.

4. Regularly play and listen to soft soothing music like the sound of waterfalls or birds chirping. This will help you to maintain a relaxing environment at all times.

5. Before you start a healing session, light a scented candle or scented incense, or both.

6. Set a fixed time for your practice and strictly follow that schedule on a daily basis.

7. Strictly practice the hand positions and healing methods for 21 consecutive days without fail. If you break the streak, you have to start again from day 1. The goal is to repeatedly do it without a day off to help form a habit. You will be amazed at how good you feel after the 21 days is complete!

Now that we have tackled all the activities that form part of the second process, you will find in the succeeding chapters other important things that you need to know about the Reiki healing system.

Chapter 11: The Impact of Reiki on Relationships

When you're young, it's easy to imagine that being in a relationship would be nothing but pure bliss all of the time. But, in reality, in spite of all the happiness and love that we feel, there will always come a point in time when relationships are tested. Furthermore, relationship problems not only test us as couples, but they also test us as individuals.

When you are extremely hurt, how fast do you heal? Do you quickly forgive, or do you hold on to anger and resentment for a long time? Everyone reacts differently to emotional pain, and so it is important to focus on the impact it has upon you. Because emotional pain cannot physically be seen it is often overlooked by society, despite the huge role that it plays in our lives.

Fortunately, the Reiki healing technique is capable of healing emotional pains. If you personally experience relationship issues and you want them addressed, you may conduct a distance healing session for yourself. You can simply perform the hand positions and techniques as discussed in the previous chapters.

Meditation Techniques for Reiki Relationship Healing

1. Make yourself comfortable in a sitting position. Make sure that you keep your back straight.

2. Make sure that you are completely relaxed by repeatedly doing deep breathing exercises.

3. Gently close your eyes and put your hands together in a praying position as you seek to become a channel for Reiki to flow within you.

4. Continue to close your eyes and allow yourself to feel the Reiki energy flowing within you, beginning from the top of your head all the way down to your feet.

5. Focus on your third eye and start thinking about the person that caused you emotional pain.

6. Now, open your eyes, reach for a pen and paper, and jot down the Reiki symbols that you can imagine might cover the person's whole body.

7. Envision yourself in front of that person and then, this time, jot down the Reiki symbols that you can imagine cover your whole body.

8. Use your imagination to continue thinking about the other person. In your mind, hug the person who caused you pain. Say loving words to them, and witness how their emotions transform.

9. While focusing on your third eye, imagine yourself living harmoniously with that person.

10. When you are ready to finish your meditation, place your hands once more in a praying position. Then, place them over your eyes – with palms down and your hands and arms positioned horizontally, and with your middle fingertips touching one another. Now, open both eyes gently.

11. Repeat this meditation technique on a regular basis, and slowly you will notice your emotional pains healing, and your relationship improving.

If the relationship ends in spite of the fact that you do the healing techniques on a daily basis, there is a big possibility that the answer to that relationship problem is to part ways for good. Not all relationships are destined to last, and Reiki can help in determining this.

Chapter 12: Addressing Negativities

Problems are something that affect everyone, no matter if they are rich or poor. Much of overcoming problems lies in your attitude towards them, and in this chapter, you will learn the significance of positivity when it comes to handling problems.

If you want to transform a major problem into a minor problem, try following these steps:

1. You are required to sit down and look for a comfortable position. Make sure that you are sitting with your back straight.

2. Allow your body to completely relax by doing deep breathing exercises.

3. Place your hands together in a praying position and start allowing the Reiki energy to flow within you.

4. Gently close your eyes and observe how the Reiki energy enters within you, starting from the crown chakra and flowing down to your feet.

5. Focus on opening your third eye and begin envisioning a blackboard where all your issues are written. If you get emotional at this point, don't worry – acknowledging your emotions is part of the process.

6. Next, envision yourself erasing everything that you have written on the blackboard. Then, mentally picture your life if all of the problems in it had disappeared.

7. Constantly visualize this positive mental image and observe how it brings you a positive feeling throughout your inner body.

8. Now, be mindful of your inner guidance because it will tell you when you are ready to finish your meditation. Once you are ready, place your hands in a praying position, rub the palms of your hands, and place them over your eyes. You may now gently open your eyes.

9. Remember to practice this meditation on a daily basis until your issues are completely healed. You are doing this meditation to attract what you want in to your life through the law of attraction.

Chapter 13: Techniques for Aura Cleansing

The aura can be described as the magnetic field surrounding every person's – and every living thing's – physical body. Auras have different sizes, depending on the person's level of spiritual growth. For instance, a small aura may mean that the person has a negative mindset, while a big aura may mean that the person has a positive mindset.

The thoughts we hold in our minds – whether they are negative or positive – have a remarkable impact on our auras. Individuals who can deeply observe and read auras know if a person has a negative or positive aura. They also know when a person changes their aura from negative to positive.

We are all familiar with personal hygiene, but there is also a thing called spiritual hygiene. This means that we should learn to keep our aura as clean as possible. In other words, our aura should be as positive as possible. A personally hygienic person washes regularly to stay clean. This is somewhat similar to a spiritually hygienic person – they practice healing techniques on a daily basis to get rid of the negativity that they feel. Being spiritually hygienic will allow a person to be happy and energetic. Their positivity will automatically attract positive people and more positive things will transpire in their life as a result.

The following is a simple aura cleansing technique that you can perform on a daily basis:

1. Sit comfortably as you keep a straight back.

2. Begin doing deep breathing exercises until you feel completely relaxed.

3. Visualize a globe of light glowing brightly above your head. Picture it moving down slowly, and surrounding your whole body.

4. Now, visualize a golden comb moving through the strands of your hair as if an invisible hand is making it move. Imagine that with every brush stroke, the negativity in your life falls down and is replaced by positivity.

5. Continue visualizing the golden comb as it moves through your hair until you feel that all negativities have fallen down.

6. Now, imagine a golden pyramid around your body as if it is a shield protecting you from any negativity.

7. End the meditation when you are ready, and repeat this on a daily basis.

Chapter 14: Augmenting Life Force Energy

Each one of us has life force energy. But let me emphasize to you that all living things have life force energy – and not just humans.

The higher your life force energy is, the happier and healthier you can be. The more happiness and good health you exhibit, the more handsome or beautiful you become in the eyes of others. Have you ever come across a person who may look rather plain physically, but for whatever reason they still seem unbelievably attractive to you? That is the power of high life force energy.

So, if you want to augment your life force energy, then here are some simple steps that you can follow:

1. Avoid cigarettes, alcohol, or any other intoxicants for that matter.

2. Eat a diet made up primarily of vegetables. When buying vegetables, make sure that you choose the produce carefully. Buy only those that are fresh and organic.

3. Include fresh and organic fruits in your diet too.

4. Be kind to every person you meet – even to strangers. Exhibit kindness without judgement.

5. Aim to constantly express your compassion and love to people, because it strengthens the life force energy. Learning to truly love unconditionally has powerful benefits!

6. As much as possible, avoid getting angry. Anger does not do you any good. It negatively affects your health and it consumes your life force energy.

7. Live with integrity. Always communicate from the heart and always express your pure intentions.

Conclusion

Thanks again for taking the time to read this book!

You should now have a good understanding of Reiki and be ready to try Reiki healing for yourself. I wish you the best of luck in your spiritual journey!

If you enjoyed this book, please take the time to leave me a review on Amazon. I appreciate your honest feedback, and it really helps me to continue producing high quality books.